Good Night
San Luis Obispo

JULIO

First edition, May 2019
Copyright © 2019 Jennifer Kirn

ISBN-13: 978-1-0771-1094-6

Published by Penciled In
5319 Barrenda Avenue
Atascadero, CA 93422
penciledin.com

Paintings by Gay Melody Sullivan, gaymelodyprints.com
Book and Cover Layout by Benjamin Daniel Lawless

The typeface used was Neutra Text TF, designed by Christian Schwartz for House Industries.
Layout was composed in Scribus 1.5.4 on a 2016 MacBook Pro, macOS Mojave 10.14

Good Night
San Luis Obispo

WRITTEN BY *Jennifer Kirn*

PAINTINGS BY *Gay Melody Sullivan*

For Declan

Your awe and wonder are contagious.
Thank you for reminding me of
the simple beauty of life.

As you grow, remember your home
with love and never forget that
if you are kind, everything else
will fall into place.

Good night to our vibrant
Bubble Gum Alley,
Good night to the moon
over Old Edna Valley.

Good night Pinots and
good night Viogniers,
Good night to the
kayakers on the bay.

Good night zebras
and good night deer;

Good night Hearst Castle and
good night San Simeon Pier.

Good night to our iconic
Morro Bay rock,

Good night to the boats
moored on the dock.

Good night to the students
of Cal Poly and Cuesta,

Good night to our town,
which hosts such exciting fiestas.

Good night to the Madonna Inn
and the Copper Café,
Good night Farmer's Market,
where we walk every Thursday.

Good night to the Mission and
the eucalyptus trees,

Good night Santa, will you bring us presents, please?

Good night to
the Fremont and
good night to the
Apple Farm;

Good night to our city
that has such charm.

Good night
Avila Barn and the
Bob Jones trail;

CORN

Good night to the boats in the
harbor before they sail.

Good night to the
Aquarium at Avila Beach.
We love to learn all that you have to teach.

Good night seals and good night whales.

We long to see your gigantic tails.

Good night to the Shell Beach Dinosaur Caves;

Good night to the
magnificent surfers
riding the waves.

Good night to the vast
Oceano Dunes,

Good night to our local bands
for playing such fun tunes.

Good night chickens and
good night swinging bridge;

Good night to the sunset
over Avila Ridge.

Good night, San Luis Obispo,
thank you for being so unique,

Good night to one of our favorite trails, Bishop Peak.

Made in the USA
Monee, IL
27 May 2022

96652797R00029